The Complete Guide to

Guinea Pig Care and Ownership

A. K. Bowen

Publication Data

A.K. Bowen
The Complete Guide to Guinea Pig Care and Ownership – First edition.
Summary: "Successfully caring for and owning a Guinea Pig"
Provided by publisher.
ISBN: 978-1-954288-91-1
[1. TThe Complete Guide to Guinea Pig Care and Ownership – Non-Fiction] I. Title.

This book has been written with the published intent to provide accurate and authoritative information in regard to the subject matter included. While every reasonable precaution has been taken in preparation of this book the author and publisher expressly disclaim responsibility for any errors, omissions, or adverse effects arising from the use or application of the information contained inside. The techniques and suggestions are to be used at the reader's discretion and are not to be considered a substitute for professional veterinary care. If you suspect a medical problem with your Guinea pig, consult your veterinarian.

Design by Sorin Rădulescu
First paperback edition, 2023

TABLE OF CONTENTS

Chapter 5

Chapter 6

Chapter 7

CHAPTER 1

Why Choose a Pet Guinea Pig?

First and foremost, guinea pigs (also known as piggies or cavies) make great pets! I have had them as a child and as an adult! Piggies are relatively easy to care for because they have a simple diet, generally require minimal maintenance, and have a relatively long life span for rodents (about six to eight years). For all these reasons, they are wonderful animals for kids whose parents want them to learn about the responsibility of caring for a pet. But of course, as with any pet, parents will also need to assume their roles in caring for a guinea pig.

"Proper guinea pig care is an adult responsibility." - **Peggy Barron from Knoxville Guinea Pig Rescue**

Photo Courtesy of
Erin Mannie

According to PETA, there are several reasons why guinea pigs do not make good starter pets for kids whose parents aren't willing to help in their care:

- Guinea pigs need time to get to know you. And some will forever prefer "hands-off" guardianship, which may be hard for a child to understand.
- Guinea pigs are messy (and require a lot of work to clean up after).
- Guinea pigs require loads of laundry. Towels used during bathing and outside playtime and fleece bedding will need to be cleaned frequently.
- Guinea pigs' teeth can be piercing. Although they typically only bite if they are sick or fear for their life, guinea pigs will bite in self-defense—and their teeth can penetrate the skin, resulting in a painful abrasion.
- Guinea pigs require monthly manicures (and you need to be incredibly careful and precise when trimming their nails).
- Guinea pigs should always be adopted as a pair. Solitary guinea pigs are often unhappy and bored. They need cage mates to talk to and play with.

But as long as a parent is willing to make up for the work that a child cannot or should not do, guinea pigs make great family pets!

> **"**
>
> *Guinea pigs DO NOT make great first pets. They are more expensive to own and require a great balanced diet of Timothy hay, Timothy pellets, food-quality lettuce, and veggies. They require a specialized exotic vet, and most of all, they require socialization of their own species and with humans. But they DO make great pets. They only bite if they are afraid for their life or if they are ill. Well-socialized guinea pigs will cuddle with their humans and make adorable sounds to 'talk' with us. A calm guinea pig is great for the physically or mentally challenged. They are cute, smart, and have their own individual personality.*
>
> JULENE ROBINSON
> *Wheek Care Guinea Pig Rescue*
>
> **"**

As alluded to by Robinson, what makes guinea pigs even more remarkable is the fact that they have different personalities. Some are lively and active, while others are more chill and laid-back. Because of this, you should work with local shelters, breeders, or pet-store employees to find the right piggie for you and your family. No matter what their personality, however, guinea pigs are social in nature, and they require daily human interaction—including petting, stroking, and playing.

They are also very vocal. They squeak when they hear you approaching, when you open the fridge, and when you give them food. Some guinea pigs even purr like cats when they are happy and curled up with you. Overall, they are very interactive animals.

Specific considerations

As previously mentioned, guinea pigs are highly social animals, and they require a lot of attention from their owners. If their needs are not met in that regard, they may become ill-tempered. They also have good memories, and they'll store poor treatment in their brains for as long as they live.

Boredom can be prevented by getting a second piggie for them to play with. It's actually recommended to get two or more animals that are already bonded. In some countries, it's even illegal to have one solitary guinea pig! However, owners should be careful if getting one female and one male, as they can make more guinea pigs if they are not fixed or spayed (neutering the male is a less invasive procedure). Of course, adding a pig to your household will only increase the amount of maintenance required.

Guinea pigs need at least one friend to interact and play with.

> " It is a myth that guinea pigs with a cage mate will be less bonded with their human owners.
>
> SARA PILGRIM
> *Companions Spay & Neuter Clinic*
> "

You will need to make sure that you do not squeeze or squish your guinea pigs. That will cause them pain and make them afraid of humans. They are relatively small and delicate. You cannot roughhouse with them

Photo Courtesy of Anne Vila

like you can with other pets—like dogs and cats. Always remember that they have good memories, so you want their association with you and your family to spark happiness, not anxiety or dread. When handling a guinea pig, always act cautiously and softly. They respond well to light pets and scratches. Some pigs will also enjoy snuggling up with you. It's best to always hold them while firmly supporting the front and back of their bodies. Their spines are very fragile, so a fall could be very detrimental to their health.

HELPFUL TIP
Rabbits and Guinea Pigs

There is a myth that rabbits and guinea pigs can cohabitate happily in the same enclosure. Unfortunately, this myth is just that—fiction. These two small pets may carry diseases that are harmful to the other and can become aggressive. In addition, rabbits and guinea pigs have different needs and communicate differently. Experts suggest keeping these animals separate if you have both as pets.

Other than properly handling a guinea pig, several other measures should be taken to keep them happy and healthy. This includes preparing for an emergency or disaster by assembling an animal-specific evacuation kit in the form of a travel cage, a food supply sufficient for about two weeks, fresh water, bedding, and medication.

> 66
>
> *Meds and supplies you should have on hand are Betadine solution, triple antibiotic ointment, cuticle cutter clippers, baby simethicone gas relief, a small bag of quality pellets (Oxbow, ZuPreem or Mazuri), a 1 ml oral syringe, and a 3 or 5 ml oral syringe. Pharmacies will usually just give them to you if you tell them it's for a guinea pig.*
>
> JULENE ROBINSON
> *Wheek Care Guinea Pig Rescue*
>
> 99

FUN FACT

Not Pigs

Despite their name, guinea pigs are not related to pigs but rodents. The Latin name for guinea pigs is *Cavia porcellus—porcellus* means "little pig" in Latin. In addition, male guinea pigs are called boars, and the females are called sows. It's unclear why these small pets were named after pigs, but some believe it's because of guinea pigs' grunting and squeaking sounds.

You should also take care to make sure that they have enough sustenance needed to survive when you go out of town for a short amount of time.

If you're considering getting guinea pigs, you should consider that they are crepuscular, which means that they semi-nocturnal (but not totally). They are mostly active in the early morning and the evening, and they will take frequent naps throughout the day. Remember that they are also very vocal, so they might be kind of loud while you and your family are trying to sleep.

A pair of Abyssinian guinea pigs

A mother sow and one of her pups

History of guinea pigs

Guinea pigs (*cavia porcellus* in Latin) belong to the rodent family. They are originally from South America, specifically the Andes Mountains. No, they are not from New Guinea or Guinea, which their name would suggest. Instead, they are thought to have been domesticated by humans in Ecuador, Peru, and Bolivia around 5000 BCE. In fact, guinea pigs continue to play an important role in Peruvian folklore, medicine, and religion. Some people believe they (especially black guinea pigs) can even diagnose illnesses. For that and other reasons, they were worshipped by ancient civilizations, such as the Moche people, who lived in Peru from around 100 CE to 800 CE in the northern region of the country. The Incan people of Peru also bred guinea pig exotic varieties from 1200 to 1500 CE.

They became popular pets in Europe after the Spanish colonization of South America, and they were especially revered among the wealthy and members of the royal families. Of note, Queen Elizabeth I of England was one of the first European enthusiasts of guinea pigs.

Pro/con list of guinea pig ownership

If you are still on the fence about whether or not guinea pigs are the right pet for you, here's a list of pros and cons to help aid in your decision.

Pros	Cons
They are cute and cuddly.	They may urinate or poop on you if you keep them outside of their cage for a prolonged period of time. (Generally, they urinate about every 15 minutes).
They squeak and purr to communicate with you.	They're nocturnal, so they may be kind of loud during the night.
They're small.	They're really delicate and must be handled with care. Parents of young children should supervise playtime.
They have longer life spans than other rodents.	Their prolonged lives should be considered in terms of the money required for food, bedding, toys, veterinary care, and medications.
They do not have to be taken outside like dogs, and they can be left at home by themselves for a short amount of time.	Their enclosures become soiled quickly and need to be cleaned out regularly.
Most crave attention.	You will need to provide daily interactions between you or your family members and the piggie. Having two or more guinea pigs is recommended. Also, you will need to get someone to come and check on them while you're on vacation.

A group of American guinea pigs

Photo Courtesy of Kelly Mastronardi

FUN FACTS ABOUT GUINEA PIGS

01 They are not pigs! They're rodents.

02 Guinea pigs create a special Pellet (it looks like their poop but it is different) called a Cecal pellet, which they eat, giving them valuable nutrients

03 They don't sweat.

04 They are vegans.

05 Babies are born fully formed with fur and teeth.

06 When they get excited, they "popcorn."

07 They secrete a white substance out of their eyes that they use to clean themselves.

08 They have four toes on their front feet and three toes on their back feet.

09 They make lots of noises.

10 Guinea pigs can learn tricks.

11 They are social and happiest when in a group.

12 Young piggies are called pups.

13 The oldest-recorded guinea pig lived to be 14 years and 10 months old.

14 They frequently take short naps instead of sleeping for long periods at a time.

8 THINGS YOU SHOULD KNOW BEFORE GETTING A GUINEA PIG

01
Guinea pigs can be active for 20 hours a day.

02
They are not agile—they're hiders but not climbers.

03
They need lots of leafy green vegetables.

04
Guinea pigs are incredibly social

05
They are explorers, and they can see you from multiple angles.

06
Due to their size, they tend to be cautious.

07
They make 11 different sounds.

08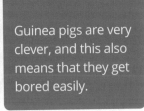
Guinea pigs are very clever, and this also means that they get bored easily.

CHAPTER 2

Where To Get Your Guinea Pig

Big Chain Pet Stores

Big chain pet stores are the first place many people think to get their pets from. This may be the most convenient option, as stores such as Petco and PetSmart can be found almost anywhere. But you should take care in educating yourself about a particular store because

some get their rodents from mills, which can sometimes mean that the animals weren't properly cared for before coming into your home. This can cause health problems (mostly respiratory issues) and premature death. Checking reviews may be especially helpful in choosing the right store.

Personally, as a young kid, I got my guinea pig, Peanut Butter Patches (he had little peanut butter-colored patches all over his body—he was the cutest!), from a big chain store. I was a child and didn't know

HELPFUL TIP

American Cavy Breeders Association (ACBA)

The American Cavy Breeders Association (ACBA) promotes responsible breeding and aims to increase public awareness of cavies or guinea pigs. The ACBA hosts annual cavy shows and is affiliated with regional clubs worldwide. In addition, this club publishes *The Journal of the American Cavy Breeders Association (JACBA)* quarterly, which is included with club membership. For more information about ACBA, visit www. acbaonline.com.

any better. Fortunately for PBP and me, he ended up living a long and happy life. But not everyone is as lucky as I was. So, it's best to always do your research and consider alternatives like local stores or breeders. Now, as an adult, I would suggest looking for guinea pigs that are available from local shelters.

> " *"Guinea pigs should not be 'purchased.' There are many abandoned guinea pigs in rescues and shelters, so there is no need to support breeders by purchasing them from breeders or pet stores."*
>
> MICHIKO VARTANIAN
> *Orange County Cavy Haven* "

As an important side note, I also want to point out that you should always be skeptical of any store that keeps females and males in the same enclosures. According to Julene Robinson of Wheek Care Guinea Pig Rescue, this is because pregnancy and birth are really hard on guinea

pig females. In fact, *"statistics on cavy births are that one out of every five sows that give birth will die during or after birthing a litter,"* she says.

Robinson noted that it's even more dangerous for underdeveloped females to get impregnated, which can happen when males and females are allowed around each other because sows can get pregnant as young as three weeks old. These young mamas often go into premature labor and produce dead or dying litters. But even if the babies do somehow live, the young mom typically doesn't have enough extra calcium (as it's being used by her tiny body to grow) to provide a litter. Regardless of who loses out on this vital mineral, either the mom or the babies, a death sentence is likely imminent for someone. So, it's just a bad situation all around that should be avoided at all costs.

Exotic Pet Stores

Like with big chain stores, you should also be careful when selecting which local stores to get your guinea pig from. Again, reviews can be particularly helpful in assessing the treatment and care of the animals that were previously bought there. Small, family-owned businesses may supply healthier exotic pets than the bigger chains because they typically have better relationships with the breeders they work with. Additionally, their employees are usually more knowledgeable and passionate about caring for animals.

Furthermore, it may be easier to develop a connection with local store employees and owners, and they can serve as a focal point if you have questions about the right foods, environment, etc., for your guinea pig. Going to a local store will also improve the chances that your pet was handled correctly before being introduced into your life. Remember, guinea pigs have great memories, and they will remember poor treatment. So, you'll want to look for piggies that already have positive associations with humans.

If you get your guinea pig from a big chain or a smaller exotic store, Susan Jones from AZ Country Cavy in Arizona suggests you ask three questions before you purchase a pet:

1. How long have you had this guinea pig?
2. Have you given the guinea pig any medications?
3. Where did you get the guinea pig?

Pregnant Guinea Pig

FUN FACT
Cavies

Guinea pigs are often nicknamed "cavy" or "cavies" because of their Latin name, *Cavia porcellus*. Cavies belong to the *Caviidae* family of rodents that is native to South America. This family also includes capybaras and maras.

She also says, *"Most pet stores will not give the guinea pigs any medications; only veterinarians will give medications if the guinea pig shows any signs of illness. Watch the guinea pig for any signs of illness. What the guinea pig may show is hiding in a corner of the cage with the head down, crusty eyes, and a runny nose. These guinea pigs will also be very thin. Most pet stores will* have an Igloo pet home in the cage. Guinea pigs like to hide in them. When you are allowed to hold the guinea pig you are looking for, take a look at the eyes. Are the eyes clear with no redness or drainage coming out of the corners? Take a look at the hair. Does the hair look shorter on one side? This usually means that the guinea pig is being picked on by one of the 'roommates' in the cage or chewing on itself. When they chew on themselves, this can be a sign of lice. The guinea pig you are holding—is it really thin, or is it big? If it is big, it means that the guinea pig is healthy."*

Commercial Breeder

Another suitable alternative is to look for commercial breeders of guinea pigs. You can find some in your area by looking online on Craigslist, Facebook Marketplace, or through a general Google search. As with the big chain and local stores, breeders should be thoroughly researched before an animal is purchased. One way to determine if the breeder is conscientious or not is to look for reviews

Mowgli

17

or testimonials from owners who previously bought animals from them on their websites.

Similar to local pet stores, breeders are often concerned with properly caring for and treating the guinea pigs from a very young age, which only makes it easier for the animals to adjust to being in your home. Also, breeders are typically available long after you purchase your pet, so you can consult them for advice if you need it.

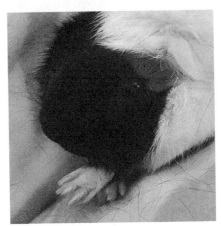

Baloo

You can also find top breeders at exotic guinea pig shows or conventions. They often bring a sample of their animals to display. These shows can give you the opportunity to form a relationship with your favorite breeders and learn more about guinea pigs in general. Sometimes breeders even take orders from people who want to purchase one of their pigs.

However, please make sure to not only pick the right breeder but also make sure he or she is local and within a reasonable driving distance from where you live. Some breeders offer to ship animals, but this should be avoided at all costs because the animals are usually contained in enclosures that are too small. You also run the risk of the guinea pig being able to escape, and the process as a whole can be detrimental to their health.

Jones says, *"If you can find a guinea pig breeder in your city, it is best to buy one from a guinea pig breeder. The reason is that you know where you bought your guinea pig from, and if you have any questions, they are more likely to know the answers to your questions versus if you got your guinea pig from a pet store."* In particular, she also recommends first-time guinea pig owners get their pets from a breeder. Jordan Heritsch from Small 4 Paws Guinea Pigs in Illinois says that if you rescue an animal, you should always make sure to ask and note its background and sensory triggers.

Guinea pig rescue/ shelter

As I said earlier, this is my preferred option for finding a pet. I'm a believer in the famous saying "adopt, don't shop." Adopting an animal is not only cost-effective, but it's also a great way to find an animal who really appreciates you, and it makes room for more animals who need to be rescued. Although rescue animals may come with the risk of behavioral problems (as they may have

I got my guinea pigs from Underdog Pet Rescue of Wisconsin

trauma from being abandoned by their previous owners), that has not been my experience.

Julene Robinson of Wheek Care Guinea Pig Rescue also agrees. She says, *"DON'T SHOP ... ADOPT! There is literally a rescue for every species and breed. Guinea pigs are the most abused/neglected/thrown-away species of domesticated pets, but they are so overlooked by society that you just don't hear about it."*

When I was in my early twenties, I rescued two guinea pigs, a bonded pair I named Mowgli and Baloo, from a local shelter. They were incredibly social animals, and I loved them very much. We had daily cuddle sessions, and they often sat with me as I studied for school. They were the first animals I had as an adult, and they taught me that I was responsible enough to care for animals with more extensive maintenance requirements.

Unfortunately, Mowgli and Baloo have since passed, but their ashes were spread in butterfly gardens, and I now have three cats (all of them are also rescues). I honestly don't think I would've ever felt comfortable caring for Duchess, Daisy, and Saffron if it wasn't for the guinea pigs I adopted before them.

I used an app called "Petfinder" to find my guinea pigs. I would recommend that you use that or something similar to find piggies available near you. However, as with all of the other options, you should do diligent research about a particular shelter you are interested in rescuing from.

10 REASONS TO ADOPT A GUINEA PIG

01 You know the guinea pig has seen a vet and is likely in good health. Also, you'll be provided with a better insight into your guinea pig's health history.

02 The rescue will probably offer you support for the rest of your pet's lifetime.

03 The rescue may take the animal back if there's a dramatic change in your lifestyle and you can no longer have a guinea pig.

04 It's more likely that the guinea pig has been handled regularly by staff and volunteers, so your bonding time may be quicker.

05 Rescues will likely give you advice on how to introduce guinea pigs to each other.

06 You will know for sure what the gender of your animals is.

07 When you adopt, you're creating space for another animal who needs rescuing, and your rescue fee will go toward helping those animals!

08 In general, it's just a good practice to support your local shelters.

09 You are actively cutting down overpopulation.

10 It's more likely that male and female guinea pigs will be kept in separate enclosures, so you may not need to deal with the complications that can come with guinea pig pregnancy and birth.

CHAPTER 3

Choosing the Right Guinea Pig

Choose wisely

As guinea pigs typically live from six to eight years, deciding to welcome them into your home is a pretty big decision. But after you decide that they are the right pets for you and your family, you'll want to be careful picking them out in terms of their overall health, temperament, and emotional connection to you.

> *You want to find a piggie that is in good health and doesn't have scabs, sores, torn ears, missing fur, overgrown teeth, or just overall doesn't look healthy. Look the piggie over carefully for lumps or bumps, which could be abscesses.*
>
> KIM MEYER
> *Austin Guinea Pig Rescue*
>
> *I recommend spending time holding your guinea pig prior to agreeing to take him/her home, so you can make sure you feel a heart-to-heart connection.*
>
> HALEY DEL VALLE
> *Bigfoot's Small Animal Rescue*

Photo Courtesy of
Lydia Zakusilov

You may also want to consider the specific breed, as some require more attention and grooming than others. Guinea pigs of certain breeds are known for being more playful and friendly than others. And because of grueling grooming requirements, guinea pigs with longer hair, like Silkies or Peruvians, are not recommended for first-time owners or owners who are not looking for higher levels of *maintenance.*

For breeds that are on the livelier side, Jordan Heritsch of Small 4 Paws Guinea Pigs recommends Teddy Guinea pigs: *"they are the most active and social; it can be very fun for new guinea pig owners to see them active in the cage."*

However Julene Robinson suggests that the American breed is the friendliest. She also says that Abyssinians are the sassiest of guinea pig breeds, as these pigs are known for having *"aby-tude."* Although I have to say, my last two guinea pigs were Abyssinian, and they were sweet as pie.

Breeds

The American Cavy Breeders Association (ACBA) recognizes 13 different breeds, but some other sources list over 20. For this book's purposes, we will just focus on the standard 13 breeds that are recognized by the ACBA. They include the following (as you will see, the "Satin" versions of the breeds simply have shinier coats):

Abyssinian/Abyssinian Satin

These pigs are known for their unique coats, which are marked with radially growing swirls known as "cowlicks" or "rosettes." To me, they kind of look like adorable emo kids from the early 2000s. Other than having an attitude, they are also known as being more energetic than other breeds, and they are easier to train due to their inquisitive natures. Prospective owners of this kind of animal need to educate themselves on the special grooming that their coats require to prevent tangling. Mowgli and Baloo were regular Abyssinians.

Alternative breed names	Origin	Size	Lifespan	Coat type	Pros
N/A	South America	**8** to **12** inches	**6** to **8** years	Rough	They tend to be very affectionate and loving after mild training.

Abyssinian

Abyssinian Satin

American/American Satin

American guinea pigs are the most common and popular breed. Their short coats require less maintenance, which is why they are desirable for first-time and experienced owners alike. In addition, they are known for being friendly and active animals. I'm willing to bet that Peanut Butter Patches was an American guinea pig.

Alternative breed names	Origin	Size	Lifespan	Coat type	Pros
Cavidse porcellus	South America	8 to 9 inches	6 to 8 years	Shorthaired	Their hair does not require regular brushing or trimming, and they are known for their floppy ears and round nose.

American

Coronet

Commonly known as Crested Silkies in the US but Coronet in the UK, this breed is the product of breeding a Silkie and a Crested guinea pig. Coronet piggies have the long, straight hair of a Silkie and a rosette "crown," like other Crested pigs have. They are known to be playful and like to engage in social activities—which is probably why they are suitable for showcasing at exhibitions or conventions.

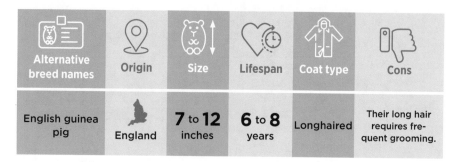

Alternative breed names	Origin	Size	Lifespan	Coat type	Cons
English guinea pig	England	7 to 12 inches	6 to 8 years	Longhaired	Their long hair requires frequent grooming.

Coronet

Peruvian/Peruvian Satin

This breed has the longest coat of any of the guinea pigs. Other than needing regular combing and grooming, these animals are known as being loving and easy to handle.

Alternative breed names	Origin	Size	Lifespan	Coat type	Cons
N/A	France	**8** to **12** inches	**6** to **8** years	Longhaired	They are high maintenance compared to shorthaired breeds and require a lot of grooming.

Peruvian Satin

Silkie/Silkie Satin

Like the Coronet and Peruvian breeds, Silkies have long coats. But their hair grows from the back of their heads and is known for being incredibly soft (hence the "silk" in their names). They are also generally gentle and shy. Owners who are on the quieter side and are willing to do regular grooming are perfect for Silkies!

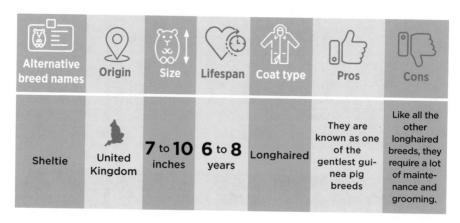

Alternative breed names	Origin	Size	Lifespan	Coat type	Pros	Cons
Sheltie	United Kingdom	7 to 10 inches	6 to 8 years	Longhaired	They are known as one of the gentlest guinea pig breeds	Like all the other longhaired breeds, they require a lot of maintenance and grooming.

Silkie

Teddy/Teddy Satin

True to their name, this breed is known for being friendly and cuddly—like a teddy bear. And although they appear to have short coats, they typically have more hair than the other shorthaired breeds.

Alternative breed names	Origin	Size	Lifespan	Coat type	Pros
N/A	Unknown (breed was found via genetic mutation)	8 to 12 inches	6 to 8 years	Rough	They are generally good-natured and have sweet temperaments.

Teddy

Texel

This is a relatively new breed, thought to have been created in England back in the 1980s by crossbreeding a British Rex and a Silkie. That is why its hair is curly, not straight like the other longhaired breeds. These pigs are known for being docile, calm, and sweet-natured.

Alternative breed names	Origin	Size	Lifespan	Coat type	Cons
Curlies	England	**7** to **12** inches	**6** to **8** years	Longhaired	Again, like the other longhaired breeds, they require a lot of labor and time to maintain

Texel

White Crested/American White Crested

As mentioned earlier, this breed is known for having a "crown" on the top of the head. It's a rarer breed of guinea pig, said to be joyful, mellow, and loving.

Alternative breed names	Origin	Size	Lifespan	Coat type	Pros
Cavidse porcellus	South America	8 to 9 inches	6 to 8 years	Shorthaired	They require less maintenance than breeds with longer hair. And the white swirl on top of their heads, which is what distinguishes them from the regular American breed, is really cute,

White Crested

Other breeds that are not recognized by the ACBA include Alpaca, Baldwin, Himalayan, Lunkarya, Merino, Rex, Sheba, Skinny, Magpie, Ridgeback, and Swiss guinea pigs

Skinny

Ridgeback

Merino

Alpaca

Lunkarya

Baldwin

Magpie

Rex

Sheba

Colorizations

As you can see from the pictures, guinea pigs come in various shapes, sizes, and colors. Here are the terms and definitions that are most commonly used to describe the coloring of guinea pigs.

- **Agouti**: Every hair changes color from the base to the tip, (this is known as "ticking") with the central part of the hair appearing the brightest. Agouti's also have a "belly band", a strip of lighter hair on their belly. There are lemon, silver, golden, chocolate, cream, and cinnamon Agoutis.

Agouti

Pink Eyed White

- **Albino**: Completely white animals with pink/red eyes.

- **Brindle**: Dark and light tan.

- **Dalmatian**: Like the dogs, these guinea pigs are white with dark spots.

Brindle

Dalmatian

- **Himalayan**: Red eyes with a white body with black nose, ears, and feet (see a picture of the breed of the same name below)

- **Mixed**: Any assortment of colors

- **Roan**: Dark hairs evenly interspersed with white

Himalayan

Roan

- **Self**: Solid-colored coats

- **Tortoise Shell**: Patched dark and light brown colors

- **Tortoise Shell and White**: Basically, the same as the regular tortoiseshell, but there's also white coloring in the coat.

- **Werewolf**: A semi-hairless skinny breed that has short, coarse, curly fur.

Tortoise Shell

Tortoise Shell and White

Store, breeder, or shelter environment

As previously stated, when looking to purchase or adopt a guinea pig, it's important for you to assess the environment it is being kept in. This will automatically tell you the level of care of the establishment you are getting a piggie from. You should look to see how neat the enclosures are kept, how much food and water are readily accessible to the animal, and how many toys are provided for the piggie to interact with.

FUN FACT

Hairless Guinea Pigs

The ACBA recognizes 13 guinea pig breeds, but several unrecognized breeds exist. Two such breeds are the hairless varieties—skinny pigs and Baldwin guinea pigs. Skinny pigs are born hairless, have a small amount of hair on their noses and feet, and may have patches of hair on their bodies. Baldwin guinea pigs are born with hair that they lose within their first few months. These hairless rodents require a warmer habitat than their hairy counterparts and may need additional skin care.

Moreover, you should also analyze the overall "vibe" of the place. You should be able to detect the intentions of the people around you within a few moments.

Inspecting each Cavy

Once the surrounding environment is assessed, the health of the individual pets you are interested in should be considered. You will want to look for visual signs of illness or poor treatment—like cuts, scabs, missing teeth, or lumps and bumps on the skin, etc. Furthermore, you should be on the lookout for overgrown nails; crusty, murky, or cloudy eyes; drooling; poor appetite; irregular shape and consistency of droppings; the appearance of being under or overweight; signs of stiffness or lameness; inactivity; and disinterest in you and any toys. Please note that it is generally normal for a guinea pig to be wary of you at first, and jumping away from your hand or light nibbling may not be cause for any concern. But if the piggie doesn't seem to warm up to you after proper handling for a while, it might not be the right pet for you.

Here are some signs of an unfriendly guinea pig at a glance:

1. Teeth chattering (the most common sign of an unhappy pig)
2. Hissing, chirping, or strutting
3. Growling
4. Fluffed up fur
5. Biting
6. Crying
7. Excessive hiding
8. Disinterest and/or staring blankly at the corner of the cage

DID YOU KNOW?
Chirping

Chirping does not necessarily mean the piggie is unhappy. There has never been a definitive decision why a guinea pig will "chirp like a canary". Some say it is because the piggie is unhappy, but I have never known that to be the case. It usually happens when the room is quiet and all of the other piggies are just grazing or napping. But no matter what the other piggies are doing, as soon as the chirping starts, all of the other piggies literally stop everything they are doing and listen." **Julene Robinson - Wheek Care Guinea Pig Rescue**

Mowgli and Baloo, two bonded boars. Seriously, how cute were they?!

Conversely, here are the typical behaviors of a happy and friendly pig:

1. Popcorning
2. Squealing
3. Purring
4. Eagerness to socialize with you
5. Not hiding
6. Nose rubbing (this is how they give kisses!)
7. Cuddling
8. Grooming (of you)

You may also want to consider which gender piggie is ideal for you. There are several things you should think about before bringing your furry friends home. They include the following:

	Female Guinea Pigs (Sows)	Male Guinea Pigs (Boars)
Size	Smaller and shorter	Larger
Weight	Lighter	Heavier
Behavior	Less active	More active
Personality	Friendly and shy	More assertive personality (and more vocal)
Aggression	Less aggressive*	More aggressive
Hygiene	Cleaner	A little bit messier
Care Required (and Cage Requirements)	Require less maintenance (they need less space)	Require more maintenance** and more frequent cleaning (they need more space)
Level of Training Possible	As they can be shy, training is not always easy	Easier to train due to personality and high level of energy
Compatibility with Others of the Same Gender	They can live peacefully among each other and do not fight often	Will often fight for dominance with other male guinea pigs***

* This is just what is generally said. Some people do not always agree with this and believe it's actually the opposite—that males are more tender, loving, and affectionate. I've only had male piggies, and I found them to be wonderful pets.

**Male guinea pigs also come with additional care regarding their private areas. You may need to take special care to clean them.

***Getting two males who are already bonded can help reduce the tension between them. Mowgli and Baloo were both boys. But they were already accustomed to each other before I met them, and they lived harmoniously with each other while in my care. I know it didn't hurt that I kept them in a large enclosure, so they always had their own space inside of it. Providing plenty of food, water, toys, and hiding spaces also aids in keeping a friendly environment among two or more guinea pigs.

However, all of this is to suggest that you should pick the healthiest and friendliest guinea pig over the "prettiest," as social piggies in good health have the highest chances of living happy and long lives with you. As Heritsch says, "Not every 'cute' guinea pig will have the right temperament."

CHAPTER 4

Setting Up Your Pet's Home

Welcoming home your guinea pig

Once you've found a location you feel comfortable getting your guinea pigs from and have found the animals that you connect with most, it's time to start preparing to bring them home. And there's no better way to welcome your new guinea pigs than having the perfect habitat established and ready for them.

The goal of setting up spaces for your guinea pigs is to eliminate the stress associated with being removed from a location in which they have previously been comfortable.

Your Guinea Pigs are best suited to live inside your house. If you have other animals in the house, you may want to consider isolating your new guinea pigs in a separate room as they initially acclimate to your environment. Then, allow each additional animal time and space to get used to the cage and the piggies—but always supervise interactions when the guinea pigs are outside of their cages.

For reference, my cats never seemed particularly interested in Mowgli and Baloo, but they would sometimes sit on top of their cage and try to swat at them. The cage was so high, however, that their paws never came anywhere close to the guinea pigs' bodies. Then, when the piggies were out and playing with me, the cats would sometimes sniff them, but they were never aggressive. Of course, I wouldn't have allowed that to happen.

Behavior of your pets

> **"**
>
> *Healthy guinea pigs should have a good appetite and produce plenty of poop. They should be active and alert and should interact with their owner and objects in their environment. It is not normal for a guinea pig to hide in a corner constantly and show no interest in food. Some other signs of common illnesses include excessive sneezing, discharge from eyes or nose, bald patches on the body (other than behind the ears or inside the front legs, which is normal), excessive scratching, or head shaking.*
>
> SARA PILGRIM
> *Companions Spay & Neuter Clinic*
> **"**

As you introduce new guinea pigs to your home, you should always observe their behavior (especially during the first few weeks) in terms of happiness and health.

Adjustment Suggestions

You will also need to do your part to make the new piggie feel welcomed and safe in your environment. Peggy Barron suggests several things about bringing a guinea pig into your home. She says, *"Guinea pigs are prey animals. Shadows looming over them are frightening, as is grabbing. Pet store guinea pigs are most likely to be frightened. Snuggle sacks are a great method of picking up the piggies. They are readily available online. Encourage the guinea pig to enter the snuggle sack while talking to it in a soothing voice. This is a job for parents or older siblings. Most guinea pigs are scared in new surroundings. Rescue piggies as well. They are accustomed to their current situation and don't understand change, new noises, scents, or other animals. It takes time and patience."*

Similarly, Michiko Vartarian says, *"Start slow and do not force your pigs to interact with you immediately. Allow your pigs to feel safe in their huts and in their new home, and then, over time, start to take them out for lap time, cuddling them in a fleece blanket so they feel safer when being held. Also, give them healthy treats while cuddling them so they learn to associate something good with something that, at first, can be frightening to them. By nature, guinea pigs are prey animals and will not always feel*

One of my cats hanging out with Baloo

safe being picked up or being social with their people, so patience is required to let them build up a trust and comfort with you slowly."

The cage

When it comes to the placement of a guinea pig's cage inside your home, as I just mentioned, they are very susceptible to extreme cold and heat. Guinea Pigs can't handle temperatures over 85 degrees, or under 64 degrees. So, you should make sure that you do not place the cage anywhere near an air- conditioning vent, heating vent, fireplace, or windows with direct sunlight. The perfect location will be a living area with a consistent temperature between 65°F and 75°F and a humidity between 40 and 70 percent. However, Susan Jones of AZ Country Cavy says "In Arizona, the humidity is much lower; 10-15% on average and my guinea pigs do just fine." The cage should be placed somewhere with good ventilation but no sudden drafts.Especially if you have a hairless guinea pig, you should avoid any area that has the potential to get windy or cold.

It's also recommended that you place the main enclosure in an area of your home that is frequently occupied by you and your family but is also relatively quiet (so you don't spook the animal) and away from

*Photo Courtesy of
Erin Mannie*

chemicals/sprays, heavy perfumes, candles, etc. According to Peggy Barron, *"[a]child's room is the worst location for guinea pigs."*

In terms of size, it's true what they say—the bigger, the better! You want to provide your guinea pigs with plenty of space to play, exercise, sleep, and explore. All of those are essential for maintaining a piggie's physical and mental health and happiness. According to Julene Robinson, a cage for two guinea pigs should be no smaller than eight square feet. She also states that pet store cages are too small. Instead, use C&C cages, MidWest Plus, or Kaytee Open Living Guinea Pig Habitats. I can't remember for sure which cage I had, but I chose the dimensions (7.5 square feet for one pig/10.5 square feet for two) suggested by the rescue I got the guinea pigs from. You can always do the same if you are unsure. Vets, of course, are also helpful in that regard.

Whatever cage you decide is best, you should make sure that it does not have plastic tubs or wire floors. Glass aquariums are also not acceptable for housing guinea pigs. Instead, enclosures made from cubes and coroplast, a corrugated plastic (like C&C cages), are best. Floors should

Photo Courtesy of Dori Jordan

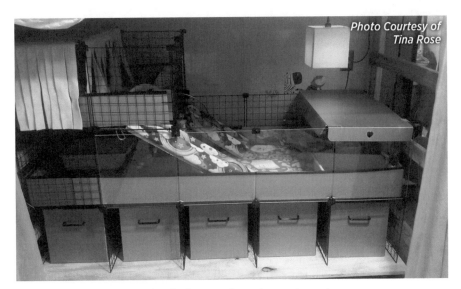

An example of a large and spacious guinea pig cage

be soft and comfy, and the sides should be wire and/or mesh to allow for maximum ventilation. As far as a roof goes, guinea pigs, unlike hamsters and other rodents, cannot climb the sides of their cages—so a roof may not be necessary. But you should make sure that the sides are high enough (especially around ramps or second floors) that the piggies cannot simply walk out of the enclosure. Guinea pigs have poor depth perception, so they need help not to fall out of their cages. A top may also be necessary to protect the piggies from other animals in your home. Remember what I said about my cats trying to swat at the guinea pigs? I shudder to think what would have happened if I didn't have that layer of protection for them.

I would also recommend you pick a cage that you don't mind looking at. I know that may sound silly, but that will only increase the amount of time you're drawn to interact with your pets. However, you should always prioritize safety over looks.

You should also factor in how easily the enclosure can be cleaned, which is very important because convenience will likely encourage you to do it more often. You can look into getting washable liners that can help speed the entire process, but items like plastic linings or bags should be avoided because your guinea pig can bite off and ingest bits of that plastic, which can lead to bowel impaction.

Bedding

After selecting the perfect cage, it must be lined with bedding, which should be absorbent, soft on the guinea pig's feet, and dust free. At first, I used the paper bedding available at the pet store. But once I educated myself more, I used fleece cloths, which are highly cost-effective because you can just wash and reuse them.

Paper bedding is dusty and holds moisture. If not cleaned regularly every other day, it can cause a very painful sore on the feet called Bumblefoot. A great alternative to fleece (which requires a puppy pee pad or some other absorbent substrate) is GuineaDad Liners. The initial outlay for two set ups is a little expensive, but as long as the care instructions are followed, they will last a long time and are much easier to clean daily with a rubber lint brush, it literally only takes a few seconds.

Photo Courtesy of Peggy Frezon

Bailey Pettit points out that getting the fleece pieces the first time may seem expensive—but you never need to buy more bedding after that! She also suggests looking up "fleece guinea pig liner" on Etsy (which is where I got all of mine) and similar websites. Of other bedding options, she says, "Paper/wood chips are SO bad for their congestion as there are a lot of dust particles given off!"*

Interior Design/ Accessories

With the cage and lining set up, now you can start thinking less in terms of practicality and more of having fun when it comes to the interior design and accessories put inside for your guinea pigs. Of course, you should always consider safety first. Some people choose to pick themes (like the forest, under the sea, etc.) for their cages. I did not do that. I just wanted to make sure that there were plenty of hiding places (fleece corner hangings and tunnels) for each of my guinea pigs, which is the

main reason for having accessories inside of the cage in the first place. It's also important to have extras so that you have replacements to use in rotation during the cleaning process.

Other pet-safe accessories include hiders (at least two per animal—or more!), cuddle cups, sleep sacks, beds with pillows, and wooden castles. Some of these can be especially fun for DIYers because you can craft a lot of them on your own, and that may be more budget-friendly than buying premade options.

Photo Courtesy of Cynthia Merrill

*Wood bedding is acceptable as long as it is Aspen or large flake kiln dried Pine

Photo Courtesy of Sheri Parsons

Toys you should never offer your guinea pig

- Exercise wheels. Guinea pigs have weak spines, so this toy is not suitable for them.
- Toys made with harmful dyes and chemicals.
- Toys made with small parts.
- Toys made with added sugars.

Susan Jones of AZ Cavy Country recommends getting a cloth covering to put over the cage at night. She says, *"You can also get a small blanket to partial[ly] cover their cage at night. Guinea pigs like to hide, and partially covering their cage will give them a sense of security."*

Food and water feeders

> *Wheek Care Guinea Pig Rescue doesn't believe in or use bowls for piggie's pellets or veggies. Bowls are human inventions. Piggies are foragers. They don't carry bowls or silverware around in the wild. We believe in trying to keep things as natural as possible. Bowls are also a great cause of dominance fighting in the cage. The dominant pig gets the lion's share and the submissive gets the left overs, which isn't always enough to sustain them.*
>
> JULENE ROBINSON
> *Wheek Care Guinea Pig Rescue*

*Photo Courtesy of
Andie and Zane Silvius*

A guinea pig sipping from its water bottle

Food bowls should be flat-bottomed but can be ceramic, plastic, or metal. No matter what you choose, however, you should make sure that the material is safe for your new pet. You may also want to get bowls that are dishwasher safe if that will give you more incentive to clean them. Preferably, at least when it comes to the pellets, you should have at least one bowl per animal in the enclosure. This will ensure that each guinea pig gets more than enough food, and it will eliminate the aggression that can come with fighting over food. When giving your cavies veggies and hay, you will want to use other dishes and holders. For my guinea pigs, I attached a trough-like mechanism on the side of their cage that was always full of hay. (Note that some owners advise against these kinds of devices, especially hay balls or stacks because they can be dangerous. Some have reported their animals getting their heads or teeth stuck in them, but I never had any problem with the rack I used.) I just gave them veggies by hand. However, I've also heard of other owners putting veggies in bowls with extra water inside if they thought their guinea pigs

Photo Courtesy of Alea Ward

were not getting enough hydration. Again, you may need to play with different methods before you find out what is best for your pet.

Speaking of water, I found water bottles to be the easiest to use, and you should probably also have at least one per animal attached to the cage. You should also make sure to get a drip-free bottle, however, because you don't want the water leaking out all over the cage while you're gone for the day. The proper device will keep the water inside and only be released when the guinea pig comes in contact with it by pushing its tongue against the little bead inside. However, I know other owners have found that their animals prefer water bowls. Maybe my boys were particularly messy, but I found that they wouldn't keep that water clean for very long, and I didn't want to discourage them in any way from drinking it. So, trial and error may be needed here. Pick one method (or use both!) and make sure that your piggie is getting enough hydration. As far as the experts go, Jordan Heritsch says, "Choco nose water bottles and Lixit ones are my favorites."

Maintenance/ Cleaning

Maintaining the cleanliness of your guinea pig's cage is incredibly important. Sure, cleaning up droppings and soiled bedding are not the most pleasant activities, but it's part of what you sign up for when you decide to get these pets. You should do a complete clean at least once a week, but mid-week "refreshes" should also be done. The thorough and mid-week cleans will vary depending on what type of bedding you use.

Photo Courtesy of Brittany Provencal

Typical Bedding

- **Total Clean** – You will want to remove all of the old stuff, clean the cage itself, and replace the lining with new, clean bedding.

- **Mid-Week Clean** – Scoop out particularly dirty pieces and poop and replace them with clean bedding.

Fleece Bedding

- **Total clean** – Remove all of the fabric pieces, clean them, clean the cage itself, and replace the lining with clean fleece.

PRO TIP
Daily spot cleaning can make these chores less demanding.

Cleaning a guinea pig cage

- **Mid-Week Clean** – Scoop out droppings and swap out pieces of fabric that appear to have been urinated on.

Food bowls and water dishes should always be cleaned on a regular basis. You will also want to clean toys and hideaways as often as needed. It may seem like a lot, but all of this cleaning is essential to keeping your guinea pigs safe because they are very susceptible to disease and infection. Especially for the more thorough cleanings, you will want to make sure your animal is out of the cage and somewhere safe—like with a family member or playing in a safe space within your sight.

Again, as with exercise wheels, please keep in mind that the balls that hamsters use are NOT safe for guinea pigs. Remember what I said about their weak spines? They don't mix well with rolling of any kind.

HELPFUL TIP
Introducing Roommates

Guinea pigs are very social and ideally live in groups of two or more pigs. Same-sex guinea pigs who have been raised together typically get along fine, but how can you introduce a new cavy to the group? The following are a few tips to help with introductions:

- **Cage size:** Experts suggest providing at least 10 square feet of space for two guinea pigs sharing a cage.
- **Bedding:** Before introductions, swap your guinea pigs' bedding so that they can learn their new roommates' scent.
- **Barrier:** Introduce your cavies through side-by-side runs or by placing their hutches beside one another.
- **Offer distractions:** When your piggies first meet each other in a neutral space, offer distractions like fresh vegetables and treats scattered around the area.

It may take several sessions for your guinea pigs to acclimate to each other. Therefore, patience and supervision are crucial for the guinea pigs' early days together.

11-STEP CLEANING CHECKLIST

01 Get your piggies out of their cage and place them somewhere safe.

02 Scoop droppings and soiled bedding.

03 Remove old hay.

04 If you use fleece pieces, put the dirty fabric into the wash (or you can wash it by hand and hang it to dry)

05 Take toys, houses, and other accessories out and clean with pet-safe sprays or soaps.

06 Remove food bowls and water dishes/bottles, discard old food* and water, and wash.

07 Clean (with the same pet-safe cleaner that you used on the toys and accessories) any surface in the cage where your guinea pig stands (floors, ramps, etc.).

08 Replace lining with clean bedding.

09 Put accessories and fresh hay back in.

10 Fill bowls, dishes, and bottles with fresh food and water.

11 Put your piggies back inside.

*This is for pellets only. Fresh fruit and vegetables should be removed after a few hours to prevent your guinea pig from potentially ingesting moldy food.

CHAPTER 5

Feeding

Like people, every guinea pig has favorites when it comes to its daily food—pellets, fruits, and veggies—and treats. So when you get a new piggie, you should offer it a variety of pet-safe foods and treats and find out which ones it likes best. And it will definitely let you know through its squeaks if it wants what you are offering. When it comes to veggies, you should avoid giving your pet cabbage, broccoli, or cauliflower because, according to Marie Crawford of Idaho Guinea Pig Friends Sanctuary, these foods can cause gas and bloat a guinea pig. Bloating is really painful and can even cause death.

HEALTH ALERT
Yellow Teeth

Teeth discoloration in guinea pigs is often a sign that something is wrong. This unsightly condition is sometimes caused by temporary staining, but you might need to take action if teeth do not return to white. Like all rodents, guinea pigs' teeth never stop growing and must be filed down through a high-fiber diet. Discolored teeth may simply be too long or a result of gum disease. If you notice your guinea pigs' teeth have turned yellow or brown, seek advice from your veterinarian for further steps.

You also shouldn't allow your guinea pig to eat nuts, seeds, dried beans, corn, peas, buttercups, garden shrubs (like hemlock or privet), lilies of any kind, nightshade, oak, avocado, onion grass, onions, potato tops, mushrooms, daffodils, foxglove, and rhubarb leaves. Other human foods like bread, cookies, candy (and sugar of any kind), breakfast cereals, dairy products, chocolate, pasta, crackers, or pickled food should also not be offered or be made accessible to your piggie.

How they like to eat

Generally, guinea pigs like to graze, which means they like having several small feasts throughout the day and night. This means you should leave plenty of food out for them at all times. And there are three basic components to their diets: pellets, hay, and fruit and vegetables.

Photo Courtesy of Peggy Frezon

Suggested foods and quantities

Pellets

High-quality pellets, espe-cially those fortified with vitamin C (because guinea pigs, like humans, are mammals that can-not synthesize their own), should be provided to your piggies on a constant basis. Pellets should be chosen that will help maintain the length of the animal's contin-ually growing teeth. According to Peggy Barron (Knoxville Guinea Pig Rescue), younger guinea pigs need alfalfa pellets, but after six months, they need to transition to Timothy pellets. In general, she

Photo Courtesy of Kelly Mastronardii

suggests Oxbow, Kaytee, or Mazuri products. She also says that older guinea pigs should be given about one-eighth cup of pellets daily while youngsters should be free-fed.

Michiko Vartarian (Orange County Cavy Haven) provides further explanation as to why piggies over six months should be limited when it comes to offering alfalfa pellets: apparently, they can cause bladder stones in older animals.

Janis Tibbetts from The Parsons Pigs says you should look at the ingre-dients of all of the food you buy, and if "ascorbic acid" (vitamin C) isn't listed, then you need to either get another product or supplement the vitamin in another form.

Hay

Guinea pigs should be provided with a mound of hay that is as large as their body every single day. Hay should make up 85% of their diet. It aids in their digestion and also helps with maintaining the length of their teeth. Peggy Barron (Knoxville Guinea Pig Rescue), recommends quality Timothy hay or orchard hay. There are other types of hay that piggies can consume, but they don't seem to like the taste of some (like brome hay), they're higher calories or hard on their stomachs (like oat hay), or they may lead to an excess of calcium (like Bermuda hay and alfalfa hay). Bluegrass hay and meadow hay are also suitable options to feed to a guinea pig.

Photo Courtesy of Dori Jordan

Fruit and vegetables

Along with plenty of quality pellets and hay, you should also provide your guinea pigs with fresh leafy green vegetables and herbs every single day. In particular, many pigs seem to enjoy arugula (aka "rocket"), dandelion greens, and snow peas. And as far as herbs go, they enjoy marjoram, borage, marigold, nasturtium, rosemary, parsley, cilantro (coriander), basil, and dill. Mowgli and Baloo seemed to favor cilantro, and they squeaked extra loudly after I gave it to them. Here's another tip: guinea pigs are amazing for getting rid of green veggies and herbs in your kitchen that

Photo Courtesy of Tina Wampler

are about to go bad. Of course, don't give them any food that has already rotted, but if you would still eat it, it's probably okay for them!

There are also other foods you can offer your pet a few times a week, including endive, carrot tops, kale, silver beet, and mint. Piggies may also enjoy fruits like apples (with no seeds!), mango, and papaya.

In particular, Janis Tibbets (The Parsons Pigs) recommends offering carrots, cucumbers, and romaine lettuce to see if your pet likes them. However, Julene Robinson suggests that carrots are actually bad for guinea pigs. She says they are too high in sugar and calcium. *"One baby carrot a week is more than enough,"* she advises.

> *Main lettuces they should get: green leaf, red leaf, and spring mix (without spinach). Lettuces and veggies that should be fed sparingly: Romaine (it is higher in calcium and recalled way to often for e coli) dandelion greens (higher in oxalates which cause sludge/stones), parsley, cilantro, kale (higher in calcium) and carrots (high in calcium). Good veggies on a daily or every other day: bell/sweet peppers, any color and raw beets. The beet leaf and stems can be mixed in with the lettuce. The bulb is higher in sugar and should be fed only a chunk every couple of days. Beets are good as a maintenance veggie for their heart, liver and especially their kidneys. It will, however, turn their poop purple! Snow peas and green beens are a good treat, but should only be given once a week.*
>
> JULENE ROBINSON
> *Wheek Care Guinea Pig Rescue*

Do you want to know something weird that guinea pigs can eat? Cardboard! I sometimes put old toilet paper rolls into my piggies' cage. Obviously, this shouldn't be considered a staple of their diet, but it's good for keeping the length of their teeth down. Toilet paper rolls also double as another place to hide inside the cage. Before you offer any cardboard, make sure it is made with food-safe ink, nontoxic glue, and virgin paper. Oh, piggies also like eating their own poop too. But they produce two types: nutritious poop (or "cecotropes") and waste poop—only the former is generally consumed. That's because it is the result of undigested fibrous food; it contains vitamins and minerals, like proteins, vitamin K,

Photo Courtesy of
Alea Ward

and B vitamins, and it has good bacteria that help the digestive system function properly.

Never feed/ toxic

Other than the foods, herbs, and plants I mentioned at the start of this chapter, guinea pigs should not be allowed to eat peanut butter, rice, xylitol (artificial sugar), dried fruits, hyacinths, columbine, ferns, azalea, anemone, geraniums, holly, mistletoe, hydrangea, honeysuckle, ivy, juniper, yew, tulips, scarlet pimpernel, and rhododendrons. Moreover, you should avoid meat and sugars of all kinds. A guinea pig's body does not process them well. In particular, Peggy Barron (Knoxville Guinea Pig Rescue), recommends avoiding all yogurt drops that are available at most pet stores.

You should also never feed a guinea pig some citrus, like lemons and limes, because they are too acidic and can cause mouth sores. And spicy peppers, rhubarbs, tomato stems and leaves, fruit pits, and apple seeds can be toxic to them.

In general, if you are unsure of whether or not a food is safe for your pet, you should either look it up on the internet—I can't tell you how many times in my life I've googled "Is _____ safe for guinea pigs"—or consult a veterinarian. It's always better to be safe than sorry!

Guinea pigs should never ingest peanut butter

Supplements

Vitamin C

As I said earlier, guinea pigs need vitamin C supplementation in their diets. Michiko Vartanian (Orange County Cavy Haven) suggests using either liquid or chewable vitamins that are designed for human children. She advises that vitamin C drops put into water are not as effective. Other experts note that such drops can change the taste of the water, and that can discourage an animal from drinking. Nevertheless, supplementing vitamin C into your pet's diet is important because it helps stave off scurvy, which causes a decline in the overall health of a guinea pig in the form of unhealthy weight loss, excessive and prolonged bleeding after a minor injury, pain and difficulty eating, difficulty walking, internal bleeding, and other symptoms.

Vitamin C is also good for their immune systems and helps protect cells from free radicals, which are molecules produced when piggies' bodies break down food, and they play a role in heart disease, cancer, and other diseases. Moreover, vitamin C is necessary for things like forming blood vessels, muscle and collagen in bones, and the body's overall healing process.

Photo Courtesy of Kaarina Nelms

Calcium and Phosphorus

Calcium is necessary for guinea pigs to build and maintain strong bones. Plus, it is required to help their hearts, muscles, and nerves function properly. Phosphorus works well with calcium, but the balance needs to be considered carefully. The ideal ratio is 1.33:1, but the amount of calcium and phosphorus an animal needs will vary and fluctuate based on age, sex, and overall health.

Iron

Iron is vital for a guinea pig's reproductive health, but it is also essential for overall growth and development—especially when it comes to the production of new blood cells and the creation of hemoglobin and myoglobin, which are both proteins that help transport oxygen throughout the body.

Potassium

Like with humans, potassium regulates blood flow, which is essential in oxygen transportation throughout guinea pigs' bodies. It also helps allocate how carbohydrates are utilized in the body, and as such, it has an important role in energy use, fighting arthritis (the inflammation or swelling of joints), and maintaining bone health.

Marigold

This supplement is also known to aid in healing external injuries and boost the immune system.

FUN FACT
Popcorn Piggies

When guinea pigs are very happy, they may "popcorn" to show you how they feel. This adorable display is usually a hop and spin in the air and looks a bit like a popcorn kernel when it pops. A guinea pig who is popcorning is a happy rodent.

Chamomile

Chamomile can help keep an excitable animal calm down

in a natural way. It has also been associated with pain management and assisting in the digestion process.

Dandelion Leaf

As an herb that is high in fiber, this can aid in digestion and in maintaining eyesight, assist the function of nerves and muscles, and promote healthy blood. Dandelion leaf can also alleviate bloating, which can be very dangerous.

Guinea pigs can eat dandelions

Raspberry Leaf

Raspberry leaf helps to support a guinea pig's metabolism because of its high-fiber content. This is important because you want your pet to be able to turn nutrition and nutrients into proper energy. And an energized piggie will popcorn and get the "zoomies," both of which are adorable to watch. High-fiber supplements can also help control blood sugar levels, which is especially essential if you choose to introduce fruits into your guinea pig's diet.

DIY food and treats

Critical Care Pellet Mash

This special food may need to be made (or purchased) if you notice that your guinea pig has stopped eating. It's a way to almost "force feed" them, and it will keep their digestive system going until their health is restored.

This is Julene Robinson's (Wheek Care Guinea Pig Rescue) recipes

1. To make your own Critical Care pellet mash, take about 1/4 cup of pellets, put lots of water on them, and nuke them in the microwave for about 15 seconds to get the pellets to soak up the water and expand.

2. Set aside.

3. Take a tomato, a pepper (color of your choice), and a carrot (or other veggie) and puree in a blender to the texture of a smoothie. (I don't advise tasting it, though!)

4. Thoroughly combine the pellet mash and the pureed veggies. Put this complete mixture into a bowl. Refrigerate till ready to use.

5. When ready to use, put about two tablespoons of the mixture in a small plastic container and thin it with orange juice, preferably hand-squeezed, unflavored Pedialyte, or warm water. Microwave until just warm and syringe feed as much as they will eat.

When hand feeding Critical Care or pellet mash, they should eat a minimum of 10 to 15 mls every 4 to 6 hours. Make sure to refrigerate any unused Critical Care. It will sour after a day or so.

If one of my piggies is on an antibiotic, I also add one poop pellet from a healthy piggie to the mixture in the small container just before I feed them as a probiotic.

Treats

In order to raise money for local shelters, some other students and I held an animal bake sale. I decided to make guinea pig treats. The recipe was as follows:

- 1 cup Oxbow Critical Care (I replaced this with hay)
- 3 Tbsp oat flakes
- 1 apple, grated
- 1 carrot, grated
- 2 Tbsp water

Preheat your oven to about 350°F.

Measure all of the ingredients out and combine. If the mixture feels dry, you can add two tbsp of water.

Guinea Pig with Treats

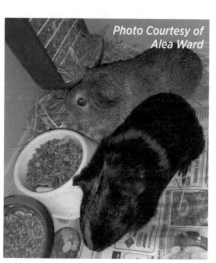

Photo Courtesy of Alea Ward

Then, ration out individual little treats (I did this with my hands) and put them on a cookie or baking sheet. Bake for 30 minutes. Allow them to cool before you offer them to your pets.

There are many other recipes you can find through a simple Google search. Making treats for your piggie is a great way to care for and bond with it!

Checklist for a new guinea pig

You can use this list to make sure that you are fully prepared for your new pet.

CHAPTER 6

Health and Physical Well-Being

Remember, guinea pigs are living creatures that are born with different dispositions, feelings, and needs. So, it's not only crucial for your pet's social well-being that you spend time with it, but it's also essential for *you* because you need to get to know every intricacy of your piggy so you know its general temperament, likes, dislikes, and more. In addition, knowing everything about your particular guinea pig will allow you to detect illness or disease much quicker—and early intervention and medical treatment are always beneficial.

Also, as already mentioned, aside from spending time cuddling or playing with your guinea pigs, you also must feed them a proper diet, maintain a clean environment, make sure they get plenty of exercise (inside and outside of their cages), and attend to any other needs they may have (like grooming).

Grooming

Brushing

Speaking of grooming, guinea pigs need your help in maintaining their appearance. In terms of their coat, shorthaired piggies require weekly brushing, and longhaired breeds will require more. Either way, make sure that you brush (preferably with a narrow-toothed comb)

Brushing a guinea pig with a fine-toothed comb is best

gently and in the same direction as the hair grows. This will remove dead hairs, tangles, and debris of all kinds. It will also give you the opportunity to check for signs of mites, and lice. In general, I would recommend giving your pet plenty of loving scratches and treats during this process. That way, it will associate the activity with fondness. And it can become a fun bonding time for everyone involved.

Bathing

Guinea pigs only require baths when their skin or hair becomes soiled with urine and feces or for the regular cleaning of their grease glands (located near the bottom of their spines), which they use to scent mark their territory. But even in those cases, they will usually only need a "butt bath," which means that only their bottoms are shampooed and then rinsed. This is done best in the sink or shallow bowl, with a towel placed on the bottom to prevent the piggie from slipping. However, you should never fill whatever you're putting the guinea pig in more than an inch or two because they do not like being submerged.

Some claim that nonmedicated soap used by humans, such as liquid Dawn or Ivory, when diluted with water, is safe to use. However, others think the harsh chemicals in those products can still cause skin irritation (even when diluted) and believe that shampoos specifically made for guinea pigs should be used.

No matter what you choose to wash your guinea pig with, you need to make sure the soap is thoroughly rinsed out (sink sprayers work well for this purpose). After the bath, towel drying is usually all that is needed. Make sure your guinea pig is thoroughly dried—they can get sick if they get chilled. However, if you have a longhaired breed and feel like it's cold inside your house, a hair dryer set on low

FUN FACT
Self-Cleaning Pigs

Guinea pigs secrete a small amount of milky white liquid from their eyes as part of their grooming regimen. This substance is a lubricant for your guinea pig's eyes and helps it clean its face.

can help dry them quicker. Of course, you should take caution when doing this because you don't want to burn your pet's skin!

When it comes to hairless guinea pigs, you should avoid giving any unnecessary baths, as it can dry out their skin, which already needs help and care (via coconut oil) to be sufficiently moisturized.

Photo Courtesy of Ashley Seweryn

An example of how to wrap your piggie after a bath

Best shampoos for guinea pigs

- Kaytee Squeaky Clean Critter Small Animal Shampoo
- Marshall Foaming Waterless Shampoo for Small Pets
- Innovet Pet Oatmeal and Honey Shampoo and Conditioner
- Johnson's Small Animal Shampoo
- Odie and Cody Natural Pet Shampoo
- Arm & Hammer Tearless Shampoo
- Fluppets Certified Organic Pet Shampoo

7 STEPS FOR THE PERFECT GUINEA PIG BATH

1. Put lukewarm water in an appropriately sized container or fill the sink (with a towel on the bottom) about one or two inches high.

2. Slowly place your guinea pig into the water and let it get acclimated.

3. Place one or two drops of shampoo into your hands and lather.

4. Apply it to your pet's body (always avoiding the head).

5. Thoroughly rinse the soap out of the hair.

6. Take the piggie out of the container or the sink and wrap it in a towel.

7. Once the piggie is dry, some owners choose to groom and apply ointments or creams (like coconut oil) to the skin.

Peruvian guinea pigs are one of the breeds that require monthly trimmings

Longhaired grooming

In general, longhaired piggies (like Silkies, Texels, Peruvians, or Coronets) who grow hair longer than three inches should get trimmings once a month. Logically, longer hair is more susceptible to becoming dirty—especially around the guinea pig's backside. And a soiled coat can cause infections and other health issues. It is safest to use round-tipped scissors to trim. With sharp ends, you run the risk of accidentally hurting your pet if it suddenly jerks or moves. If your guinea pig is especially skittish during grooming, you should constantly offer food and treats while you cut the hair. There are plenty of tutorials online that demonstrate how to give your guinea pig a haircut—and of course, you can always ask your vet for tips.

Nail trimming

You will also need to make sure that your guinea pig's nails are trimmed. In general, this needs to be done every month or every two months. Young, less active piggies and those fed nutritionally balanced diets tend to grow their nails faster. On the contrary, more active pigs tend to wear their nails down. Their nails should be trimmed with clippers meant for cats. I used a scissor style, as shown in the illustration. You should never attempt to cut your guinea pig's nails unless you've been adequately shown how to do so by a professional. Going to your vet or watching a video from a reputable source can help with that.

The task of clipping is best done by two people—one holding the guinea pig safely and close to their body, the other actually doing the trimming. But if you don't have assistance, you can always hold the guinea pig in your lap or gently wrap its body in a towel and hold it under one arm. Just make sure that its back half and front half are always equally supported. One nail should be cut at a time, and you should be very careful not to cut too close to the blood supply (known as the quick). Again, watch videos or ask your vet how to identify this on your animal's nails.

However, if you do accidentally nick the quick and the nail starts bleeding, you can apply a styptic powder or a styptic pencil (both of which are available at pet stores). Cornstarch or flour can also be used like this. You can also gently press the nail against a bar of soap or beeswax. If none of that stops the blood, gently press a paper towel against the affected nail for a few minutes. Always make sure that the bleeding has stopped completely before placing your pig back into its cage.

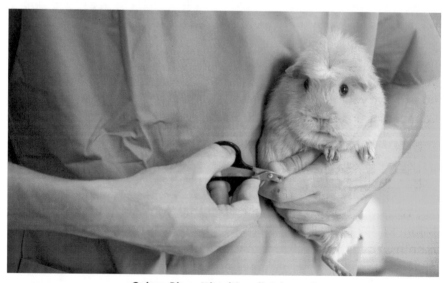

Guinea Pig getting it's nails trimmed

Anal sacs

According to Susan Jones (AZ Cavy Country), *"When male guinea pigs get older, you will need to clean their anal sac at least every two weeks. The anal sac of a male guinea pig sometimes will fill up with bedding, hair, and/or poop. You can use a cotton swab and mineral oil to clean out the anal sac."* Becky Wilson from Metropolitan Guinea Pig Rescue in Virginia supports that. She says that, in particular, older male guinea pigs who have not been neutered need to have their anal cavity cleaned every day.

Not all experts agree on that. Instead, some experienced guinea pig owners believe that you do not need to clean the sacs unless you specifically notice a problem or impaction. Like everything else, consulting a veterinarian would be best to get definitive advice.

Toothbrushing

Unlike other pets, guinea pigs do not require regular toothbrushing at home or by a veterinarian. Instead, as we've already discussed, you will need to provide hay and wooden materials to keep their continually growing teeth a healthy length. The crumbly dry pellets are not enough. If you notice that your piggie is not munching on its hay, you should bring it to a vet as soon as possible. That, along with drooling or appearing to be in pain when eating, could be a sign of tooth root impaction, which is like wisdom tooth impaction in humans (pretty painful). Moreover, you should also provide vitamin C supplements daily to keep teeth and gums healthy.

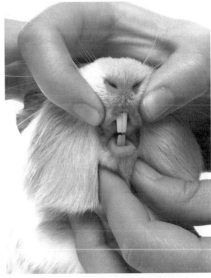

Guinea pigs are prone to overgrown and misaligned teeth

Dyeing their hair

This is a pretty contentious topic among the guinea pig community, and some seem to think that when you use the right products (100 percent animal friendly), it's completely harmless. Others, like me, aren't huge fans of dyeing the hair and fur of animals in general. Something about it makes me feel sad because they obviously didn't make that choice. I don't know. It just seems frivolous and pointless. If you feel the need to dye your guinea pig's hair, please do as much research as you can to find the least harmful product.

Physical exercise

Inside the cage

When inside their enclosure, guinea pigs need to be stimulated with toys such as balls and chews to interact with and exercise with. Your pets might not like some of the toys you get, but that's okay. Just observe them and see which ones they interact with the most, so you'll be more informed during your next shopping trip. Boxes and ramps can also help them get their energy out. You can also hide treats around the cage for them to find.

We've already covered this, but this is another reason why the cage should be as big as it possibly can be. You want to encourage your pets to jump and run around inside of it, and that won't happen if they don't have enough space. Make sure that you don't overcrowd the cage with too many toys and accessories. Always consider that they require more open space than not.

Outside the cage

Ideally, a guinea pig should get three to four hours of free-range play every single day. Having said that, they should never be outside of their

Photo Courtesy of Anne Vila

cage unsupervised. You don't want your pet to get access to wires that it can chew on or other hazards around your home. If you can't always watch your piggie, then you should get some kind of large, gated area (baby gates can work well for this). But you'll have to also make safety considerations with these in terms of placement away from the dangers I just mentioned and if you have other animals in the house.

Toys like tunnels and other toys should be accessible, as just as inside the cage; these items will encourage movement and exploration. When I had Mowgli and Baloo, I bought separate cloth tunnels for them to play with in my living room. In terms of a gated area, my apartment was pretty small, and a bunch of baby gates would've taken up a significant amount of space. Instead, my boyfriend and I would sit on the ground with our feet touching in a circle, and we'd watch and interact with them as they played. My guys weren't super active, though—I don't know how that would work with pets that were more energetic and liked to zip around.

I should also mention that some guinea pigs—especially those newly introduced to you and your home, at least in my experience—will be tempted to run and hide under beds, couches, refrigerators, etc., so you should take care to block off those areas if you can. It can be really hard (and time-consuming) to lure the piggies back out. This also leaves them helpless against other animals in the house.

Something else to keep in mind is putting towels down in the areas your guinea pig has access to outside of the cage. This will catch most of the pee or poo when your piggies do their business.

Photo Courtesy of Natalie Krasner

Ailment/ Disease

As I said before, detecting signs of a guinea pig's ailments and getting these treated by a professional is critical. However, as Bailey Pettit (Guinea Pig Rescue Foster Parent) mentioned, guinea pigs are prey animals, so they hide their illnesses very well. That's why it is important that you get to know the ins and outs of your pig's personality, preferences, and typical mannerisms. Pettit continues, *"Watching their hair, poop, pee, and any changes in behavior is very important."*

You should also look out for signs of a reduced appetite or difficulty eating, weight loss, drooling, increased thirst, fluctuations in the consistency of droppings, constipation, patchy fur/hair loss, bloody skin, dental problems, raspy breathing, and growths on any part of the body. It's best to get into the habit of daily "check-ups" that include a thorough scan of your pet's body. This can be done while you're engaging in cuddles, so the piggie might not even notice it's happening.

These daily checks are even more important as your guinea pig ages. Pettit says, *"Listening for signs of pain is really important. UTIs, bladder stones, and cancer are all things senior guinea pigs can suffer from. Watching their urine for blood, making sure their poop is regular (not too small or big), and (listening to make sure that) you don't hear crying when they are trying to potty is another big thing."*

Sara Pilgrim (Companions Spay & Neuter Clinic) recommends adding consistent weighing of your guinea pig to these checks. Specifically, she says, *"Weighing your guinea pig weekly is a good practice since weight loss can be an early sign of illness. This is especially important as guinea pigs get older and become more susceptible to age-related illnesses. If weight loss or any other symptoms of illness are noted, it is a good idea to take your guinea pig to a veterinarian for a check-up. Make sure to find a veterinarian who is experienced in treating exotic animals since many veterinarians see mostly dog(s) and cats, and their health needs are very different from those of a guinea pig."*

Becky Wilson (Metropolitan Guinea Pig Rescue) adds, *"A scale is very important to weigh the guinea pig weekly. Guinea pigs tend to hide their illnesses. Often a downward trend in weight is the first indication that something is wrong."*

Common ailments guinea pigs suffer from

Respiratory infections

- Pneumonia is one of the most common diseases that a guinea pig can suffer from. It is caused by bacteria, such as Bordetella and Streptococcus. Stress, overcrowding, pregnancy, and the presence of other illnesses increase the risk of a piggie coming down with pneumonia.

Diarrhea

- Guinea pigs have sensitive gastrointestinal GI tracts. They have a specific natural population of "good" bacteria in their GI tracts, but when this normal bacteria is altered or becomes unbalanced with "bad" bacteria, diarrhea can occur.

> **HEALTH ALERT**
> *If something with the piggie looks wrong, sounds wrong, smells wrong or if the piggie isn't acting normal, it is an emergency and veterinary care should be sought immediately.* **Julene Robinson – Wheek Care Guinea Pig Rescue**

Scurvy (vitamin C deficiency)

- As mentioned before, guinea pigs cannot produce their own vitamin C, and if they are not provided with supplementation, they can develop scurvy—which can result in a rough coat, lack of appetite, diarrhea, reluctance to walk around, pain, swelling in the feet and joints, and hemorrhages and ulcers on the gums or skin.

Tumors

- Guinea pigs can develop various tumors, but they most commonly occur on the skin and in the mammary (breast) area.

Photo Courtesy of
Emily Schmidt

Abscesses

- Infected swelling that contains an accumulation of pus and bacteria can affect lymph nodes, skin, muscles, teeth, bones, and internal organs. When these develop, they must be surgically removed. A round of antibiotics will also likely follow.

Piggies can also suffer from urinary problems, barbering (chewing of the hair), and pododermatitis (aka "bumblefoot," in which sores develop on the bottom of their feet).

** A guinea pig that is suspected of developing the problems mentioned above (or any other disease) should be seen as soon as possible by a veterinarian. **

In order to further educate yourself and get advice from experienced owners, you can join online chat groups, such as on Facebook, and guinea pig-specific websites like *Happy Cavy*, *GuineaDad* (I really love this website

FUN FACT
Unique Feet

Guinea pigs have fourteen toes, with a different number of toes on their front feet than their back. A guinea pig's front feet each have four toes, while their back feet have just three. This adaptation might be advantageous for tunneling, something that guinea pigs do for survival in the wild.

in general!), or *Yummypets*. This can be a helpful way to get to know fellow piggie lovers and ask for insight on how to properly care for your pet. It can also be a good source for health information. However, please know that guinea pigs can get sick very quickly, and it's best to always take them to a professional if you have doubts about their health.

In the same vein as Pettit, Haley Del Valle (Bigfoot's Small Animal Rescue)says you should always be on the lookout for crusty or watery eyes, coughing or wheezing, discharge from the nose, sores on the feet, lethargy (or low activity—especially if the animal is known for being particularly active), and drooling. These may be signs your guinea pig should immediately see the vet.

Choosing a Veterinarian

Things to consider when picking the right veterinarian

1. **Look for clinics that are specific to small animals** (some typically only see dogs and cats). Specifically, exotic vets/vets that commonly see rabbits (as rabbits and guinea pigs are similar animals) are best. In my experience, a quick look at a clinic's website will give you insight into the types of animals they treat. (It's also a good idea to look up where the closest emergency/24-hour exotic vets around you are.)

2. **Get a recommendation.** This is another instance where being part of an online community of others who love guinea pigs can come in handy!

Photo Courtesy of Naevia Rosa

3. **Check credentials.** You want to make sure that your piggie is being treated by the best and most caring professional possible. In order to determine that, you can visit the American Veterinary Medical Association's website (AVMA) to look up a particular vet and see their experience with guinea pigs. Other resources include the American Association of Animal Hospitals or your state veterinary association.

4. **Visit several clinics before finalizing your choice.** Getting the "vibes" of a particular clinic is really important. If you don't automatically walk in and feel that the people have a passion for animals

and genuinely care for the health of your pet, it probably isn't the right place. If you don't want to take the time to visit, you can always look online for testimonials from other people. You can also consult an online group if there are members who live around you.

5. **Inquire whether pet insurance plans are acceptable and if credit card payments are allowed.** Some vets offer discounts if their bills are paid through the company's insurance program, so it may be beneficial for your wallet to ask. Asking whether credit card payments are allowed may also be necessary—especially if you are slapped with an unexpected bill.

MY FIRST VET VISIT

Quick story time about taking my guinea pig to the vet

I had to take my piggie, Mowgli, to the vet, and I was lucky enough to find a small animal hospital right down the road from my house. I noticed a weird growth on his skin when we were cuddling, and I was worried that it might be a tumor or something else that would require medical intervention. Luckily, it was deemed to be nothing of concern. But I was happy that I took him in to know for sure. I can't remember precisely how much it cost, but I'm sure it was under $50.

I knew my vet was right for me because when I walked into her room, it was covered with guinea pigs—the wallpaper, the art, etc. It was all guinea pigs. I felt like I was in heaven! I could also tell right away that she genuinely loved cavies, and she handled Mowgli with a gentle and respectful touch. Of course, she also praised how friendly and happy he seemed, which certainly didn't hurt. I felt so proud of my boy! I hope you have a similar experience if your guinea pig needs expert care.

What will your veterinarian do for you?

- Perform a physical examination and run any diagnostic tests (such as blood work, Mendelian Genetics testing, and urinalysis)
- Based on a diagnosis, medications may be prescribed, or surgeries may be done.

It is typically recommended to take your guinea pig to the vet at least once a year. However, senior piggies may need to be seen more frequently. And, of course, if you notice changes in behavior or signs of illness, you should take your pet in to see a professional. Vet bills can be expensive, and if your clinic does not accept credit card payments, you should consciously set aside a good chunk of money for regular check-ups and emergencies.

CHAPTER 7

Mental/Emotional Health and Bonding!

Like us, guinea pigs need interaction, socialization, and excitement to enrich their mental and physical health. Therefore, if you aren't 100 percent committed to spending quality time with your pet, a guinea pig might not be right for you. The impact of stress and boredom can lead to physical ailments. Also, you really should consider having at least two animals so that your pet will have a constant companion. However, whether or not you have one, three, four, etc., piggies, you still need to spend time with them to make sure they are happy and healthy as possible.

Play and bonding (with you and cage mates)

If I haven't convinced you yet, I'll say it again—guinea pigs are social creatures, and they enjoy human interaction. That may include petting, stroking, cuddling, and playing. But you should take it slow. Remember, they are prey animals, so they may retreat or hide from you at first. You should never remove them from a hiding area. Instead, be patient and gentle. They need to learn that they can trust you and that you are not going to hurt them. The more you spend time with them, the more you will build that trust. And once your relationship has been solidified, you should handle your pets at least once a day. My favorite thing to do with my piggies involved placing them in a cuddle sack and petting them until they fell asleep next to me on the couch after a long day. Getting them to purr was so incredibly satisfying!

Janis Tibbetts (The Parsons Pigs) reiterates, *"Guinea pigs are personable; that is, they bond with their human caretaker. The more you hold them and talk to them and pet them, the more they trust you and respond to you."*

ASK THE EXPERTS!

Bonding your Guinea Pigs

JULENE ROBINSON
Wheek Care Guinea Pig Rescue

Julene Robinson of Wheek Care Guinea Pig Rescue has plenty of experience in bonding guinea pigs. These are her expert recommendations:

Unless they have previously been together and already know each other, two or three guinea pigs will need to be introduced to each other in neutral territory the first time they meet. This introduction is a critical phase for your piggies to get along and bond into a happy family. Done correctly, they will most likely be friends for life. There is always the possibility that two piggies may just never get along, but that is rare. Immediate friendship is also often elusive. As with humans, friendship is not something that is just automatically there; it has to be cultivated, with trust being earned. An introduction that ends with no one being hurt is always off to a good start. There are many methods of introductions, and I will just list a few of the ones that I have used and know work.

When introducing guinea pigs, especially males of similar ages, it is best to introduce a new piggie to your cavy family in neutral settings, usually the floor.

The first method is to start out with one person holding one pig and a second person holding the other pig some distance apart, and then release them both and let them "find" each other. I always like to have a big pile of hay in the middle. Friendships tend to form better over food. Don't we do the same? We go to dinner with someone because it's a neutral setting and a chance to get to know someone better without our own personal space being compromised. Some people put a little hand lotion on their hands and then hold the pigs so that they both "smell the same."

There are five steps to this type of introduction. The first step is when the piggies are let go to find each other. Then, once they realize there is a stranger in their area, they will each want to be the boss. They will start out by sniffing each other to check on the sex of the intruder. Males and females alike will both want dominance over the other. The first step is often overlooked, and the pigs go straight to step two.

The "fun" starts once the pair or trio become aware there are strangers in the area. Someone has to be the boss and, depending on the age and size of the pigs (the sex of the pigs is irrelevant since both sexes seem to follow the same routine in bonding and bossing), this is the critical step. Each cavy wants to appear to be "bigger" than the other. They will yawn to show how big their teeth

Photo Courtesy of
Francine VanHorn

are, chutter their teeth, rumble strut (stomp from side to side in place, chuttering their teeth), chase, paw at the ground like a bull, and mount each other. This show of dominance can last from just a few minutes to more than an hour.

It is during this time that minor bite injuries may occur. UNLESS THERE IS MAJOR ARTERIAL BLOOD LOSS OR DAMAGE, DO NOT SEPARATE THEM! They are doing what guinea pigs do in their world. It looks brutal to us, but they know what they are doing. At this point, don't try to pet, touch, talk to, or intervene with the piggies. You may be the one to get bitten. Your gentle little guy isn't himself at that time and has very little clue as to his surroundings.

Once all of the dominant behaviors have subsided, the piggies enter the fourth step, which is when the piggies will lie down some distance apart from each other. At this point, they have pretty much worked out the hierarchy and are testing the waters. Even though all looks calm, just leave them alone. Don't talk or pet them or interfere in any way. They aren't done yet!

In the fifth and final step, they will move to lie side by side, facing in opposite directions. The intros are pretty much finished at this point, except for an occasional mock nip. Leave them alone to rest for several minutes. Use this time to get their cage set up and ready for them. If this initial introduction is done anywhere other than their final home destination (such as adding a second or third pig from a shelter or rescue; usually that shelter or rescue will do the initial introductions to make sure there is a basis for a lasting bonding), put the newly introduced pigs into a large plastic laundry basket lined with a fleece blanket and a nice mound of hay. The ride home with this method is helpful because it makes the pigs huddle together.

When you get the pigs home, put them into a large C&C or MidWest cage with a nice pile of hay and no Igloos for them to hide in. It is at this point that I advise the humans to leave the room and let the piggies do what they do naturally. It's almost a repeat of the initial meeting. Usually, in an hour or so, they can be given their

Igloos back and left to adjust to their new life and friends. From this point on, unless there are SEVERE wounds, do not separate them. Minor butt bites and face nips are normal and natural. Just clip the fur from around the wound, clean it out (a bite wound has bacteria in it that can cause infection), and apply Neosporin or antibiotic ointment several times a day. Keep the wound open, as bite wounds must heal from the inside out. Hopefully, in a few days, all will be good.

Another method, and my personal favorite, should only be done by someone with experience handling guinea pigs and is a little gentler way to introduce piggies. First, I bathe the piggies at the same time so that they can huddle together in the sink ("simple stress" is a great bonding agent!), and with warm water and very smelly gentle shampoo, give each pig a bath, being careful not to get any water in their ears or up their nose. Next, dry them off with a dry towel. Then, with a larger dry towel folded in half, with the fold toward your chin, put the cavies side by side, facing your chin on the towel. Then fold the bottom half of the towel up, ensuring that they can't fall through the bottom of the towel. Then fold both the left and right sides of the towel over the piggies, swaddling them tightly. (They look like a piggy burrito!)

Hold them like this until they are just about dry. I just sit and hold them, giving treats and just talking and stroking them. The stress turns to relaxation. It will take about an hour, but the piggies will start to get restless and move around. At that point, unwrap the towel and start to towel dry them to get them a little drier. After holding them for a while unwrapped, they should be more comfortable with each other and can then be put in a clean cage with lots of hay and left to get to know each other. As with the other method, unless there is serious bodily harm, do not separate them. This usually works fairly well.

Also using this method, if I am introducing males, I might throw in one more step just before I give them a bath. I check and clean their anal sacs with a Q-Tip.

The introduction process may work instantly or may take several sessions. Patience is the key. The one thing you want to remember is that skirmishes are normal. As long as there is no MAJOR blood loss (we are talking arterial spray, large gaping wounds, eye wounds), DO NOT SEPARATE THEM! This is the biggest mistake people make when trying to introduce pigs. Guinea pigs live in a hierarchical society. Someone must be boss, and trust me, telling them who is in charge doesn't work. They have to fig-ure it out themselves. These minor skirmishes are their way of doing that. It looks frightening to us, but they have been around for millions of years, doing things their way. The humans stepping in because we are frightened of their skirmish won't help solve their "boss" problem.

When introducing a baby pig to an adult pig (always make sure they are the same sex!), it's relatively easy because there is no real question as to who is going to be the boss. The adult pig, for now, will tell the baby the rules. There will be some mounting (both males and females do this), and the baby will try to hide or run, but the adult pig will not harm the baby. This behavior usually only lasts 15 or 20 minutes, and then things will calm down.

Photo Courtesy of Ashley Seweryn

Adolescent pigs (espe-cially boys) when being introduced to an adult pig will try to test the waters to see how far they can get. They know they aren't going to be the boss, but it's like a 15-year-old boy pushing an adult male to see how far he can go before getting his butt stomped. Unless the adult male is pretty much a coward, the adult male will still be dominant, and the youngster will learn his place ... for now! It's not uncommon for babies or young males to try a little later for dominance once their hormones are telling them that they are "the stuff." If it happens, just let it go and treat any wounds. Above all, do not separate them unless it becomes life-threatening.

In 23 years of rescuing guinea pigs, there have only been a few times when I've had a male that I couldn't bond with another male. Since piggies are social animals and thrive when with friends, if a male is too dominant for another male (and I am a firm believer that all piggies should have a friend or two), then the best solution is to get the male neutered, and after the proper three-week waiting period, give the male a girlfriend.

It's unusual for a male to be so aggressive that it can't get along with another male, so neutering also serves not only as a way to change their behavior by cutting out the hormones, but it also helps to make sure there isn't a physical reason for the aggressiveness. On one occasion, I had an aggressive male that I got neutered, and when they opened him to do the neuter, there was a raging testicular infection that, if left untreated, would have killed him. Another boy that was aggressive went in for the neuter, only to find out that he had an overabundance of hormones, and they were bombarding his brain. If he hadn't been neutered, this would also have killed him.

So, to wrap up, male-to-male bonding is definitely possible. The bonding will eventually be successful if done correctly and with patience and the understanding that they are guinea pigs and not humans (we need to leave our "human" feelings out of the equation).

Again, you should always consider having at least two of these pets, and you need to allow them to bond (if they aren't already bonded when you get them). I have only ever gotten animals that were already accustomed to each other.

Proper handling

Bonding with your guinea pig will only be possible if you know how to properly handle it. Piggies need to feel safe and secure with you at all times. I already commented on this, but to reiterate—you should make sure that the front and rear of their bodies are fully supported at all times. You should never hold them under their arms or shoulders. Instead, one of the best ways to hold them is by placing them on a special pad and placing a hand on top of them. I can't remember what the particular product pictured to the left was called, but similar items can be found on Esty by typing in "guinea pig snuggle pad." Or you can place them on your chest or lap. Suffice it to say, guinea pigs like to feel secure and protected at all times. You should never place them on their backs.

Sara Pilgrim (Companions Spay & Neuter Clinic) says, *"You should support their body with both hands when lifting them from the cage and bring them close to your body as quickly as possible. A good way to carry them is to place all four*

Another good way to hold a guinea pig—supporting its body on one hand and arm and placing the other on top

of their feet against your chest with your hands supporting their rump and back. They will feel much safer and struggle less when their body is supported in this way. Never pick up a guinea pig by the scruff of the neck or allow the body to flail as it is lifted since this may cause the piggy to injure its back."

Petting

Like most animals, guinea pigs like being petted by their human companions. Many like to be gently scratched behind the ears and under the chin. They also like being stroked from the neck to the rear. Make sure you always go in the direction of their hair; they will not react positively to being petted against the grain. And offering food while you pet your piggie will only positively reinforce the experience. You will know if you're doing something right when you get your guinea pig to purr or coo. Bites and other adverse reactions will cue you into things you are doing wrong or that your particular guinea pig does not like. Again, make sure that you take physical interaction with your pet slowly, and be patient as a new guinea pig gets used to you and learns to trust you.

Fun ways to bond

Other than cuddling and petting your guinea pigs, you can also play with them. Some like to play catch with balls and other toys, and some enjoy a light game of tug-of-war. It's also fun to make a food maze for them. That will ensure they are getting sufficient nutrients while enriching their minds. You can also play with them using tunnels, tubes, and chew toys. Spending time with them will educate you on the play style that each piggie likes the best. My boys were

Photo Courtesy of Tina Wampler

pretty laid-back in general, so our playtime was usually just cuddling and petting. Baloo sometimes liked playing tug-of-war—but he soon grew tired and just wanted to chill out with me. They were my constant companions while I watched TV or studied for class.

If you have more rambunctious piggies and have a particularly busy day, you can just let them roam around your bed or desk at the end of the day. But, of course, they should always be closely supervised because a fall could be life-threatening (remember their weak spines). Also, never let them freely roam around unsafe areas—such as places in your home that have a lot of electrical cords or other hazardous items for a guinea pig to chew on or be exposed to.

Training

Guinea pigs can be trained. I personally never tried anything specific, but other owners have had success in teaching them to come when called, push a ball, give a kiss, spin in a circle, and jump through a hoop. If you want to teach your guinea pig a trick, you should be persistent, repetitive, and use food as reinforcement. Of course, you should always have patience.

Some piggies can even be potty trained. Some owners place litter boxes inside their guinea pigs' cages. According to *wildharvestpets.com*, here are five steps to litter training your pet:

1. **Figure out where it likes to urinate.** Guinea pigs typically urinate in the same spot.

2. **Set the litter box in that identified spot.** Since the smell of urine will already be in that location, and because you've already seen a pattern in your animal going to the bathroom there, it's the perfect place to set the litter box. You can pick up a litter box made for rodents from a local pet store or create your own.

3. **Reward your pet.** Offering treats when your guinea pig goes to the bathroom in the litter box will only encourage that behavior in the future.

4. **Get involved with the training.** Guinea pigs have small bladders, and they need to go to the bathroom approximately every 15 minutes. So, it can be tricky teaching them to use a litter box. However, looking for signs—like fidgeting or backing up—that they need to pee and then placing them in the litter box can help. Of course, consistently reward with a treat as reinforcement.

5. **Don't scold your guinea pig.** Again, it can be difficult to potty train your piggie, and it may take some time. Be patient and never yell, shout, or demean your pet if it takes longer than you anticipated.

Litter Box Training

DIY Litter Boxes

I've never attempted to litter box train any of my guinea pigs, but if I were to do it in the future, I'd probably just buy a product designed for them at my local pet store (as I assume this is the safest and most effective option). But that's just me. Here are several DIY options for people who are inclined to make their own:

Vinegar Water Bottles

Vinegar bottles—especially large ones like you can get from Costco—can be used as litter boxes. You just need to cut off the bottom and sand the edges. However, you should be sure that your guinea pig doesn't chew on the plastic.

Casserole dishes

These ceramic dishes are great when serving as a guinea pig's litter box. You can use any dish (on the smaller side) that you have around your house, or you can probably look for a cheap one at your local thrift store. You just want to make sure that the sides are not too high—your piggie won't be able to get inside.

FUN FACT
Sleeping With One Eye Open

Don't be alarmed if you notice your guinea pig sleeping with its eyes open; this is a natural adaptation and doesn't indicate anything wrong. This unusual behavior is most likely an evolved trait to help guinea pigs avoid predators in the wild. Many guinea pig owners have observed this common behavior and report that their pets rarely close their eyes fully. When awake, guinea pigs have a remarkable field of vision of up to 340 degrees— one of the widest in mammals.

Newspaper

You can also fashion newspaper into a litter box, or you can simply line it in a specific area of the cage (like pictured above). You need to be careful with this option because it's dangerous for piggies to chew on dyed paper.

Other helpful tips for litter box training

- When you're starting out with the training, you should scoop up any droppings that are outside of the litter box and put them inside. This will help your guinea pig start to realize that is where it's supposed to go to the bathroom.
- Whatever you decide to put inside the litter box (aspen shavings, paper pellets, etc.), it should be a different material than the rest of the cage. That will assist in designating that area for your pet to urinate and poop in.
- If you decide to use an actual box or container of some kind, you should teach your guinea pig how to jump inside of it. You can do that by luring it inside with its favorite veggies or other treats.
- You can encourage your pet to go inside the litter box by putting hay, food bowls, and toys inside (or near). Of course, you need to make sure that there is enough room for the actual piggie in

Introducing a younger cavie to an older one is easier because there's no question as to who is boss

there. You should make sure that you are regularly cleaning the litter box; otherwise, your guinea pig might be deterred from using it.

- And yet another reason to have a large cage—you might want to have multiple litter boxes around (especially if you have more than one animal—which you should!) because each guinea pig may have different places that it favors.

 QUICK TIP : *Whatever you decide to train (or not to train) your guinea pig to do, just remember that at the very basic level, your pets just want to spend time with you. Their mental and emotional health is just as important as their physical well-being.*

CHAPTER 8

Interpreting Body Language and Communication

Body language

Spending lots of time with your guinea pig will also give you an understanding of the movements it makes and what each jump, flick, and lunge means. But of course, there are general actions that most piggies make.

Positive gestures and noises

Every guinea pig I've ever come across has always "popcorned," which means that it jumps in the air (resembling popcorn popping in a machine). It's typically done when an animal is feeling happy. It can also be a sign of fear, but that's rare. Not only is it adorable, but it's probably also an indication that you are doing a great job at caring for your guinea pig. I've seen guinea pigs popcorn when humans approach their cages with

Photo Courtesy of Erin Mannie

food or treats or when a new, fun item is added to their enclosures. Other positive postures include licking (a way of grooming, which I mentioned before) and sprawling out, which indicates that your piggie is comfortable while relaxing near you or on your lap.

Happy noises

The sounds that a content guinea pig makes include the following:

- **Chutting** (aka "clucking"). Guinea pigs make similar noises to what a mother hen would make when they are interacting with you or their cage mates. It's indicative that they are having a good time.

- **Purring.** Like cats, guinea pigs purr when they are content and comfortable while cuddling up with you.

- **Cooing.** This sound typically communicates reassurance. It's a sign of affection that piggies make when around their humans or their young.

- **Snoring.** Snoring is also a sign that your guinea pig is particularly comfortable when snuggling with you. However, it's important not to confuse this with the wheezing and clicking while breathing that I mentioned in the respiratory illness section.

- **Whistling/wheeking.** Sometimes it is involuntary, but guinea pigs can whistle when they are excited about something (especially when you are approaching their cage with food). If you've ever been around a guinea pig before, you know exactly what sound this is. *"It's also the noise guinea pigs make to get your attention", according to Melissa McGee from Guinea Pig City in Pennsylvania.*

FUN FACT
Oldest Guinea Pig

According to the Guinness World Record, the oldest guinea pig was named Snowball and lived 14 years and 10 months. Snowball died in 1979 in Nottinghamshire, UK. Another long-lived cavy was Bear, a guinea pig who lived 14 years and died in 2021. The average life span of a domestic guinea pig is five to seven years, while wild guinea pigs generally live only one to four years.

Four ways your guinea pigs show they love you

1. They let you pick them up.

2. They nibble at your shoes, feet, or hands.

3. They eat food directly from your hand (and it's even better if your pet lets you pet it while it eats).

4. They "wheek" when you come in the room (a sign that they enjoy your company).

Photo Courtesy of Dori Jordan

Guinea pigs love having time with their human companions outside of their cage

Negative gestures and sounds

Postures that may communicate to you that your guinea pig is unhappy include backing away when you're trying to pick it up, fidgeting or biting you while being held, freezing in place (which indicates that it is scared or startled by something), strutting (moving side to side on stiff legs, which can be an act of dominance), tossing its head into the air (which is how your piggie can ask you to stop petting it), and standing on two legs (especially when accompanied by teeth-baring, this can be a sign that your guinea pig is feeling aggressive).

Angry or aggravated noises

When a guinea pig is annoyed or fed up, it may demonstrate the following sounds:

- **Teeth chattering.** Unlike its happier companion noise, when the teeth become involved, it's a way for your piggie to say, "Stop that!" It is an aggressive vocalization.

- **Purring or rumbling.** I know I said this was a good noise, but if it's higher pitched, this sound can indicate annoyance. Furthermore, a "short" purr can be indicative of fear or uncertainty.

- **Hissing.** Similar to other animals like cats, a guinea pig will often hiss when it feels threatened or upset.

- **Shrieking.** A piercing squeak is a call of alarm in terms of fear or pain that a guinea pig experiences.

- **Squealing.** Your guinea pig will make this sound when it is unhappy or distressed. Squealing typically happens when a piggie feels bullied or is actually bitten by cage mates.

- **Whining.** Just like humans, a guinea pig whines when it is annoyed or dislikes something going around in its environment.

- **Chirping.** Although this is often said to be the least understood noise that guinea pigs make, it seems to happen when a piggie is removed from its family.

A guinea pig exposing its teeth

Neutral gestures and sounds

Some of these have already been listed as positive or negative, but they are repeated here because sometimes the postures and noises a guinea pig makes can be indicative of nothing at all. These include:

- **Mounting.** This is either a reproductive stance (when it happens between a male and a female), or it can be a sign of dominance within a guinea pig's social structure (this often occurs between females).

- **Scent marking.** Piggies will rub their chins, cheeks, and hind ends on items and surfaces that they wish to mark as theirs. However, urination may also serve this purpose.

- **Sniffing.** As prey animals, their eyesight is not necessarily the best, and they rely heavily on their other senses to understand their surroundings. As such, they use their noses and sense of smell to acclimate to their environments and to get to know other guinea pigs (like smelling each other around the nose, chin, ears, and backside).

- **Raising their heads.** This can be a sign of dominance when a head is raised around cage mates. However, this can also just be an indicator that your pet has heard or smelled something that surprised it.

- **Rumbling.** This noise is deeper than a purr, and a male guinea pig may make this sound when trying to mate with a female. It's part of what is called the "mating dance."

- **Running away from your hand.** Again, as prey animals, guinea pigs are naturally cautious and defensive. So, it is normal for them to avoid your hand when you first try to pick them up. Just give your pet patience and pick it up slowly and gently.

- **Yawning.** Like the raising of the head, yawning can be a sign of dominance—but it can also be a sign that your piggie is comfortable and ready for a snooze.

One of the things I miss most about Mowgli and Baloo is the noises they would make. They would always "wheek" whenever either my boyfriend or I opened the fridge—especially when they could hear us opening the veggie drawer, which usually meant we were getting some cilantro (their favorite treat) out for them. I also miss hearing them purr as we cuddled together on the couch. Heck, I even miss their love bites, which were sometimes a little painful, but I knew they were just being playful. I also miss seeing them popcorn. They did this when they were excited and, most frequently, when we walked through the door of our apartment.

FAMOUS GUINEA PIG

Guinea Pigs in the White House

President Theodore Roosevelt, the 26th president of the United States, enjoyed the company of many animals in his life. In addition to Roosevelt's dogs, snakes, birds, and a badger, he owned a handful of guinea pigs. The first of these guinea pigs were gifted to the family in 1893. The Roosevelts' guinea pigs' names included Dr. Johnson, Bob Evans, Bishop Doan, and Father O'Grady.

If you think guinea pigs are the right pet for you, I'm really excited for you to bring your own furry friends home and experience their unique personalities, temperaments, and noises!

CHAPTER 9

Taking Care of Senior Guinea Pigs

Some professionals say a guinea pig is generally considered a "senior" when it reaches four years old, but others say it is when it is five. Either way, about halfway into the typical life span of piggies (seven or eight years), they are considered to be older. And they often require special care and consideration as they age. Of course, all animals will progress and show signs of aging differently and at different times; this is just a general guide. Getting a guinea pig means that you are in for the long haul—which will hopefully include you taking care of the animal in its later years.

Bodily and mood changes

Aging guinea pigs are likely to lose muscle tone, fur, and weight*. They can also demonstrate behavioral changes, like showing less interest in walking up ramps, popcorning, exercising as a whole, etc. Think about it: older humans react similarly and limit the movements of their bodies when they start to experience aches and pains. Cavies may also stop activities like grooming themselves and chewing on wood to keep their teeth shorter. When that happens, you will need to step in and perform or encourage those tasks on a frequent basis. In terms of tooth overgrowth, you can try sprinkling fragrant herbal blends (but please triple-check that they are safe for guinea pig consumption!) on hay to entice the senior piggie to eat it. And please refer back to the grooming section of this book if you need suggestions and help in that area!

Again, just like older people, senior guinea pigs are more fragile, and their hygiene and overall cleanliness are of utmost importance when it comes to preserving your pet's quality of life.

Medical attention required

Senior guinea pigs can develop a number of ailments, including arthritis (typically in the knees) and GI, dental, and urinary tract problems.

Depending on gender, they can also develop specific issues. For example, sows (females) who have not been spayed might develop ovarian cysts. These cysts can grow and eventually burst if left untreated, jeopardizing the guinea pig's life. On the other hand, boars (males), as I've alluded to before, may require regular cleaning of their anal sacs to remove the accumulation of feces if they lose the ability to do so themselves.

Please keep in mind that as prey animals, guinea pigs hide signs of illnesses as best as they can, so you may want to bring a senior piggie to the vet in increased intervals as it gets older (even if you don't notice any change in its body or mood) just so a professional can evaluate it and rule out any illness.

Older guinea pigs will likely need to be seen by a veterinarian more frequently

Environmental changes

You will likely notice your senior guinea pig sleeps more than when it was younger, and you should accommodate for that by providing plush bedding and other comfort items that will promote blissful sleep. But again, please remember that you should never crowd a cage, no matter how old your pet gets.

Senior piggies can lose their eyesight with age, so you might want to consider converting two-story enclosures into a single-story. Moreover, avoid moving furniture, food bowls, water bottles, etc., around too much because your guinea pig may rely heavily on previous routines to find these items.

Dietary considerations

Other than the hay tricks previously mentioned, there are other things you may need to adjust when it comes to your guinea pig's diet. For example, you may want to measure out the amount of pellets you are offering to avoid bladder stones, and you will want to monitor exactly how much food (and water) your pet is consuming.

Other things to consider

If you initially had two or more guinea pigs, and the others have since passed, leaving you with a sole older guinea pig, you should consider giving it another playmate. Lonely guinea pigs get depressed and slowly lose their will to continue living.

And if you have any other concerns about your senior piggies, you should never hesitate to reach out to your local vet!

Depending on how old your guinea pig is (especially if it's getting close to seven or eight years), you may want to start preparing yourself for its natural passing. This is incredibly sad, but death is a natural part of life. And after your piggie dies, you should try to be thankful for the time you were able to spend with it and remind yourself that you gave it the best life you possibly could!

*Regularly weighing senior pigs is essential, as weight loss is often one of the first signs that something is wrong (although it might not always be cause for concern—only a vet can make that determination).

Photo Courtesy of Tina Rose

Made in the USA
Columbia, SC
06 February 2024

31534592R00061